9000967330

D1159711

MAJESTIC HORSES

# MUSTANGS

*by Pamela Dell*

Published in the United States of America by The Child's World®
PO Box 326 • Chanhassen, MN 55317-0326
800-599-READ • www.childsworld.com

**PHOTO CREDITS**
© AP Photo/Jeff Barnard: 21
© Bettmann/Corbis: 16
© Catherine Karnow/Corbis: 25
© franzfoto.com/Alamy: 7, 8, 26
© The Granger Collection, New York: 15
© J. C. Leacock/Alamy: 19
© Juniors Bildarchiv/Alamy: cover, 1
© Mark J. Barrett/Alamy: 11
© Momatiuk–Eastcott/Corbis: 4, 12
© Nancy Greifenhagen/Alamy: 22

**ACKNOWLEDGMENTS**
The Child's World®: Mary Berendes, Publishing Director;
Katherine Stevenson, Editor

Content Adviser: Weezee

The Design Lab: Kathleen Petelinsek, Design and Page Production

**LIBRARY OF CONGRESS CATALOGING-IN-PUBLICATION DATA**
Dell, Pamela.
  Mustangs / by Pamela Dell.
     p. cm. — (Majestic horses)
Includes bibliographical references and index.
ISBN 1-59296-783-3 (library bound : alk. paper)
1.  Mustang—Juvenile literature.  I. Title. II. Series.
SF293.M9D45 2007
599.665'5—dc22                                          2006022646

# TABLE OF CONTENTS

Spanish settlers called these horses *mesteños* (meh-STAY-nyos). It meant that the horses had no owners. Over time, the word became "mustangs."

A thundering sound fills the air. Dust rises from the ground. A herd of horses is galloping across the plain. No one owns these horses. They are free. They are mustangs!

Mustangs are free-running horses of western North America. These horses do not have an easy life. No one takes care of them. No one finds them food or water. They must take care of themselves. That is why these horses are so smart and strong.

◀ Years ago, the American West had lots of mustangs like these. At one time, there were two million of them!

Mustangs are often called "wild" horses. But an even better word is **feral**. Wild animals have always been wild. They have never been owned by anyone. But feral animals are people's pets that got loose. Mustangs came from horses people owned. Some of the horses got loose. They formed herds. They had babies. Over time, the horses got used to living on their own.

Feral mustangs try to stay away from people. But if they are caught, they can get used to people. They can learn to carry riders. If trained, they can make wonderful pets.

"Mustang" makes people think of something fast and wild. The name has been used for a fighter plane, a sports car, and sports teams.

This "Medicine Hat" mustang has a mostly white body with a dark cap. Some Native American groups believed that these horses' markings kept the rider safe. ▶

Mustangs came from a mix of horse **breeds**. They come in all shapes and colors. Most of them are small. They have thick, heavy bodies and big heads. Their backs are short. Their legs are short and strong.

Mustangs that live free often have scars. They get cuts and scrapes. Sometimes they get in fights with other mustangs.

A horse's height is measured from the **withers** to the ground. Most mustangs are 56 to 60 inches (142 to 152 centimeters) tall. A horse's height is also measured in *hands*. A hand is 4 inches (10 centimeters). Most mustangs stand 14 to 15 hands high. Some are as small as 13 hands or as big as 16 hands. For their size, mustangs are fairly heavy. Most weigh 750 to 1,000 pounds (340 to 454 kilograms).

◀ You can see the different colors in this mustang's mane and tail. You can also see how heavy and strong its body is.

9

You can find mustangs in just about every color and pattern. Many are **dun** or **roan**. Others are white, black, brown, **bay**, **chestnut**, or other colors. Some have splashes of white on their faces or legs. Others have small spots or big patches of color.

Mustangs' tails are set low on their bodies. Their manes are long. Sometimes their manes grow long enough to reach their legs.

Mustangs' hooves are hard. These horses can walk on rocky ground without getting hurt. They hardly ever have the leg and foot problems other horses have.

Free-running mustangs often have lots of hair. It keeps them warm in rain, snow, and wind.

These mustangs show lots of different colors! The horse in the middle has the bay coloring. The horse on the right is chestnut. ▶

# ★ NEWBORN MUSTANGS

In the wild, mustangs live in herds. A herd might have several **mares** and their **foals**. The herd is led by a **stallion**. He is the foals' father. Mustang herds move around a lot. The mares give birth quickly. The foals can run soon after they are born.

In the wild, many foals are born during the winter. In cold areas, the foals have thick, shaggy coats. The thick hair keeps them warm.

Mustangs take good care of their foals. At first, the foals drink only their mothers' milk. As they grow, they start eating grass and other plants. They learn how to stay alive. They learn how to get along with other mustangs. Most foals stay with their herd for one to two years. Then they leave to find herds of their own.

◄ This beautiful mare is keeping a close watch on her foal.

When Europeans arrived, North America had no horses. But the Europeans brought lots of them. Spanish, French, and English settlers brought different kinds. Some of the horses got loose. Native Americans caught some of them. But others were never caught. They became feral. These feral horses gathered into herds.

Some herds had mostly Spanish horses. Others had different breeds. The babies were mixes of breeds. Over time, other settler's horses kept getting loose. These newcomers mixed with the feral horses, too.

Some herds of mustangs still have mostly Spanish blood. They did not mix as much with other breeds. They are some of the most beautiful mustangs.

**14**

This painting shows Spanish explorers in 1540. The leader of the group was a man named Francisco Vásquez de Coronado. ▶

Many people thought mustangs were pests. The mustangs ate grasses that cattle could eat. People even hunted the horses for sport.

Feral mustangs faced many dangers. But they were smart. They learned how to live in the wild. They were watchful, brave, and fast. And they had few animal enemies. Their numbers grew quickly.

By the 1800s, everyone in the West was after the mustangs. Ranchers wanted them for saddle horses and cow ponies. Native Americans wanted them, too. Feral horses had to be taught to carry riders. People often taught them in hard, cruel ways. But these horses often kept their wild spirit. They tried to buck riders off. Sometimes they ran away—even years later.

◀ This drawing is from the 1800s. It shows a cowboy trying to ride a wild mustang.

In the early 1900s, the U.S. had about 2 million wild mustangs. People thought that was too many. They killed mustangs to get rid of them. By 1970, there were only about 17,000 mustangs left.

Today, there are nearly 32,000 mustangs running free.

But some people worked hard to save the mustangs. They passed laws against killing them. They set aside areas where mustangs could live free. They kept track of how many horses these areas had. Sometimes an area had too many. Earlier, the extra horses would have been killed. Now the government started finding people who would adopt them.

This wild mustang herd lives in Oregon. ▶

# WHAT ARE MUSTANGS LIKE?

Living in the wild has made mustangs smart! But they are different from other horses. Most horses grow up around people. Feral mustangs are not used to people. They are used to being free. They try to stay away from danger. People need to make friends with them gently. Being mean to mustangs makes them want to fight back. It makes them not trust people.

Mustangs often live to be 30 years old. That is old for a horse!

Once mustangs trust people, they make wonderful pets. They are strong, brave, and friendly. They do not need to be fussed over. They work hard to please people. But they still have minds of their own!

This trainer worked with her mustang for many months. She was gentle and calm. The mustang now feels safe around her. ▶

# MUSTANGS AT WORK

Old paintings and pictures show mustangs at work. These horses carried Plains Indians on buffalo hunts. They helped ranchers herd sheep and cattle. They carried people up mountain trails.

Today, mustangs are still doing some of these jobs. They make excellent saddle horses and cow ponies. Their short backs and great strength help them carry heavy loads. Mustangs are used for trail riding, camping, and rodeos. They do not appear very often in horse shows. But some people train them for jumping and other **contests**. And mustangs are great for riding and racing long distances.

Some people ride mustangs in *gymkhana* (jim-KAH-nuh). Gymkhana games and races are fun for everybody. There is even a "slow race"—the slowest horse wins!

◀ This mustang is being ridden by an actor. The actor is wearing clothes of long ago. He is helping to show people what the Civil War was like.

23

Extra mustangs are still being removed from government land. People have given thousands of these horses new homes. First the horses must be "gentled." That means getting them used to people—gently! Once they trust people, they can learn their new jobs. Adopted mustangs have done well at all kinds of jobs. Some work with children who have never been around horses. Others have become police horses. Some help find people who have gotten lost or hurt outdoors. And many have become well-loved family pets.

There are still many mustangs in need of good homes. The government is always looking for people to adopt them.

This mustang is being trained to lunge (LUNJ). The horse learns to walk in a circle around the trainer. It learns to understand the trainer's commands. The trainer always handles the horse gently. ▶

# MUSTANGS TODAY

Free-running horses are found in many parts of the world. But they are not mustangs. Mustangs are found only in North America. Once, America's free-running mustangs were almost gone. They are not out of danger yet. But many people are working to help them. They are working to save places where the mustangs can run. And they are finding homes for mustangs that must be caught.

Australia has more feral horses than anyplace else in the world. Australians call their free-running horses *brumbies*.

About half of America's free-running mustangs live in Nevada.

Mustangs running free are a wonderful sight. And they are a big part of America's story. With luck, they will be with us for a long time!

◀ This mustang is living free in Wyoming. It looks strong and healthy.

## ✦ ✧ ★ BODY PARTS OF A HORSE

1. Ears
2. Forelock
3. Forehead
4. Eyes
5. Nostril
6. Lips
7. Muzzle
8. Chin
9. Cheek
10. Neck
11. Shoulder
12. Chest
13. Forearm
14. Knee
15. Cannon
16. Coronet
17. Hoof

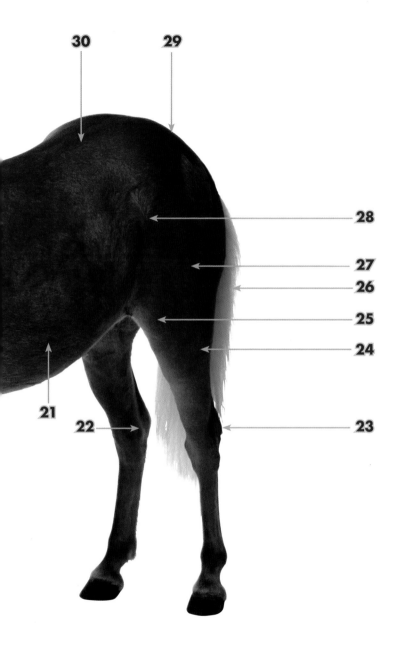

18. Pastern
19. Fetlock
20. Elbow
21. Barrel
22. Chestnut
23. Hock
24. Gaskin
25. Stifle
26. Tail
27. Thigh
28. Point of hip
29. Croup
30. Loin
31. Back
32. Withers
33. Mane
34. Poll

# GLOSSARY

**bay (BAY)** A bay horse is brown with a black mane and tail. Many mustangs are bays.

**breeds (BREEDZ)** Breeds are certain types of an animal. Mustangs are a mix of different horse breeds.

**chestnut (CHEST-nut)** A chestnut horse is reddish brown with a brown mane and tail. Many mustangs are chestnuts.

**contests (KAHN-tests)** In contests, people or animals try to win by being the best at something. Mustangs do well in some kinds of contests.

**dun (DUN)** A dun horse is a grayish yellow color with a black mane and tail. Many mustangs are duns.

**feral (FEHR-ull)** A feral animal is one that has gotten away from its owners and gone wild. Mustangs are feral horses.

**foals (FOHLZ)** Foals are baby horses. Mustangs take good care of their foals.

**mares (MAIRZ)** Mares are female horses. A mustang herd often has several mares.

**roan (ROHN)** Roan horses are a solid color with a few white hairs. Some mustangs are roans.

**stallion (STA-lyun)** A stallion is a male horse. A mustang herd is led by a stallion.

**withers (WIH-thurz)** The withers is the highest part of a horse's back. A mustang's height is measured at the withers.

# TO FIND OUT MORE

**In the Library**

Budd, Jackie. *The World of Horses.* Boston, Kingfisher, 2004.

Cowley, Joy, and Layne Johnson (illustrator). *Where Horses Run Free: A Dream for the American Mustang.* Honesdale, PA: Boyds Mills Press, 2003.

Featherly, Jay. *Mustangs: Wild Horses of the American West.* Minneapolis, MN: Carolrhoda, 1986.

Gentle, Victor, and Janet Perry. *Mustangs: America's Wild Horses.* Milwaukee, WI: Gareth Stevens, 1998.

**On the Web**

Visit our Web site for lots of links about mustangs: *http://www.childsworld.com/links*

Note to Parents, Teachers, and Librarians: We routinely check our Web links to make sure they're safe, active sites—so encourage your readers to check them out!

# INDEX

**About the author:** Pamela Dell is the author of more than fifty books for young people. She likes writing about four-legged animals as well as insects, birds, famous people, and interesting times in history. She has published both fiction and nonfiction books and has also created several interactive computer games for kids. Pamela divides her time between Los Angeles, where the weather is mostly warm and sunny all year, and Chicago, where she loves how wildly the seasons change every few months.